Learn to Sew: Kids

My First
Hand Sewing Book

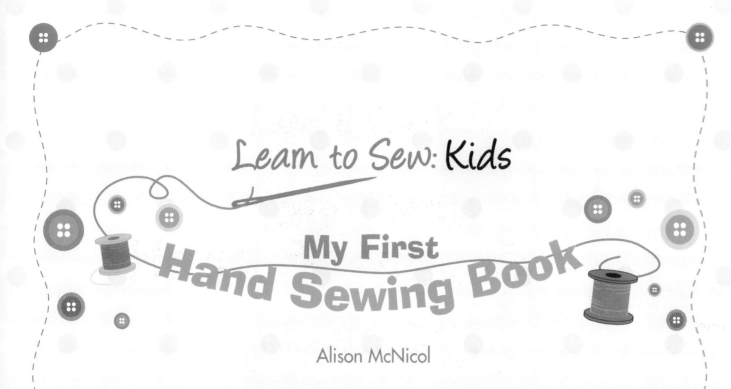

Learn to Sew: Kids

My First
Hand Sewing Book

Alison McNicol

Learn to sew and make cool stuff!

A Kyle Craig Publication
www.kyle-craig.com

First published in 2010 by Kyle Craig Publishing
Text and illustration copyright © 2010 Alison McNicol
Design and illustration: Julie Anson

Contents

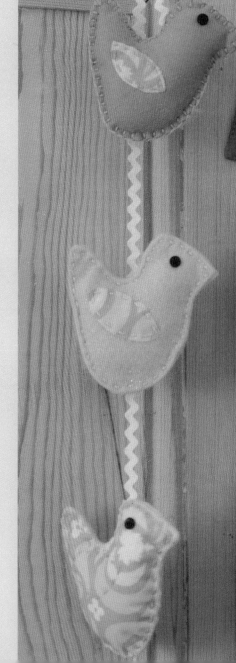

Alison and some of her pupils

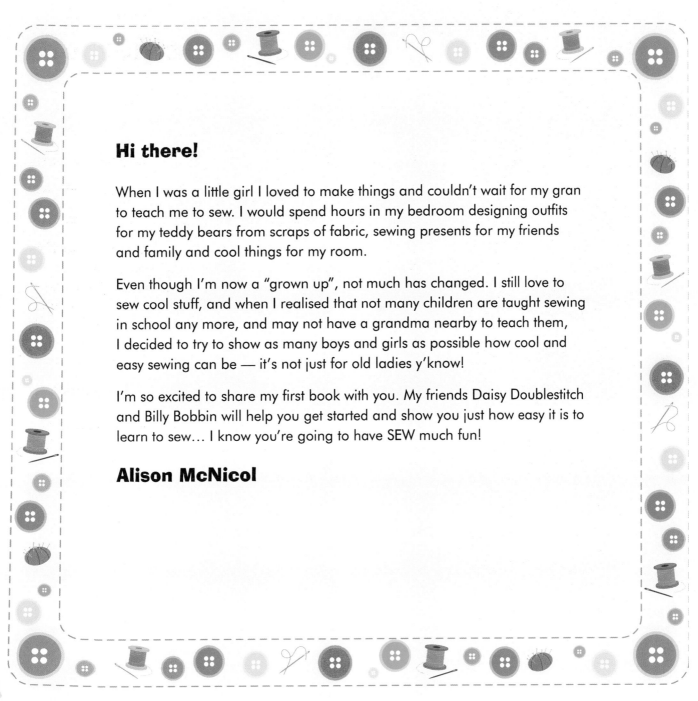

Hi there!

When I was a little girl I loved to make things and couldn't wait for my gran to teach me to sew. I would spend hours in my bedroom designing outfits for my teddy bears from scraps of fabric, sewing presents for my friends and family and cool things for my room.

Even though I'm now a "grown up", not much has changed. I still love to sew cool stuff, and when I realised that not many children are taught sewing in school any more, and may not have a grandma nearby to teach them, I decided to try to show as many boys and girls as possible how cool and easy sewing can be — it's not just for old ladies y'know!

I'm so excited to share my first book with you. My friends Daisy Doublestitch and Billy Bobbin will help you get started and show you just how easy it is to learn to sew… I know you're going to have SEW much fun!

Alison McNicol

Your sewing kit

Before you can start sewing, there are a few things you'll need, and it's a good idea to have a sewing box to keep all these bits and bobs in — that way you'll know where to find everything when you start a new project. There are lots of lovely sewing boxes out there, but even an old cookie tin or ice cream tub will do.

I also like to keep a separate box or bag for all my bits of fabric and ribbons so they won't get tangled up with pins and threads.

Be very careful with sharp scissors, and always keep pins and needles in a pincushion or a scrap piece of felt when you're not using them, and if there are younger children around, be sure to keep these sharp items well out of reach.

Tape measure
Keep one handy for taking measurements

Scissors
Have one pair for cutting paper patterns, and another sharp pair for cutting thread and fabric.

Sewing thread
Use this thread for sewing things up or sewing on buttons and beads.

Embroidery thread
This thicker thread is great for decorative stitches and blanket stitch. Use a needle with a larger eye.

Ribbons and trims
You can never have too many ribbons and trims in your sewing box!

Buttons and beads
Start collecting these to use in lots of projects.

Needles and pins
Keep these safely in a pincushion when not in use. You will need different sizes of needles for different types of thread.

Fabrics and felt
We use felt in a lot of projects in this book, plus some cotton fabrics for appliqué.

Skills

There are quite a few different sewing skills to learn to help get you started. The more you practise these — like threading your needle — the easier they will become! You can use skills like appliqué and sewing on a button for LOADS of different projects...are you ready to get started?

How to...
Thread your needle

How to choose thread and how to thread a needle are the very first things you must learn when sewing! Threads come in all colours and thicknesses, and needles come in all different sizes for different jobs.

STEP 1

Choose a needle that's right for the thread and fabric you're using. The hole for the thread is called the eye. Is it big enough for your thread? Is the needle sharp enough to pass through your fabric easily?

STEP 2

"How much thread should I use?" With the bobbin in one hand and the end in the other, unwind until your arms are outstretched, then cut. Always use this amount, even for a small job, as you don't want to run out too soon!

STEP 3

Hold your needle just below the eye. Rest your wrist on the edge of the table to help keep your hand steady. In the other hand, hold your thread, close to the end. If it's a bit fluffy, snip the end to blunt it, and wet it. Pass the thread carefully through the eye.

STEP 4

Pull one end of the thread through the needle until the thread is the same length on both sides (unless you're using fat embroidery thread). Tie a knot at the very end and smooth both strands of thread together.

How to...
Sew on a button

Sewing on buttons is easy when you know how!
You can use buttons on your clothes, or even to decorate things!

STEP 1
Decide where you want your button to be and bring your needle up through the middle of that area from the back of the fabric, so that your knot is hidden at the back.

STEP 2
Now make a double backstitch to secure your thread on the fabric before you add the button.

You use a double backstitch for LOTS of different things!

Make sure your needle does the in and the out move in one go.

STEP 3
Now bring your needle and all the thread up through one hole of the button. Next go down through the other hole, again pulling thread all the way. Do this at least 4 times or until the button no longer feels wobbly when you tug it.

STEP 4
On the underside of the fabric, underneath the button, do another tiny double backstitch and you are finished!

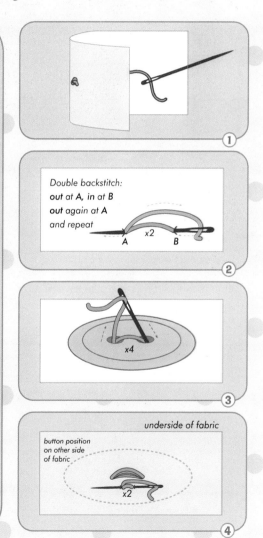

①

Double backstitch:
out at A, in at B
out again at A
and repeat
A x2 B

②

x4

③

underside of fabric
button position
on other side
of fabric
x2

④

How to...
Use pins

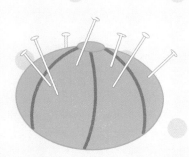

You use pins to attach patterns to your fabric before you cut it, or to hold your fabrics in place as you sew.

STEP 1
When pinning a pattern to your fabric, you must use lots of pins all around the outside of the pattern to hold the paper shape to the fabric.

STEP 2
Now the pattern is secure enough for you to cut out a neat shape.

Tip!

Make sure your fabrics stay flat when you pin them. Check they're not bumpy before you cut!

STEP 3
Once you have cut out your shape, you need to remove the pins and paper, and then pin your fabrics back together. This holds it in position while you sew. Now you can sew it together!

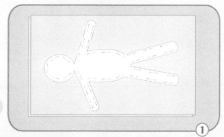

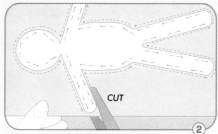

CUT

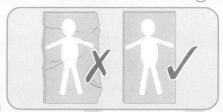

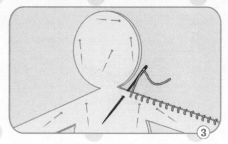

How to...
Use a pattern

You use paper patterns or templates to help cut the correct shapes or pieces for the project you are making.

STEP 1
The paper pattern has a solid line to show you where to cut around the paper pattern, and the number will tell you how many of this shape to cut. First cut out the paper shape carefully. Be careful not to cut inside any lines.

STEP 2
You must then pin the shape carefully to your fabric. Be sure not to waste fabric so think about how you position each shape.

STEP 3
Cut out your fabric shapes, remove the paper, and pin them back together ready for sewing.

STEP 4
On some patterns the dotted lines show you where to sew and the Daisy heads show you where to begin and end. You can use a pencil to mark these on your fabric.

> When you see me, don't forget to always begin and end with a double stitch!

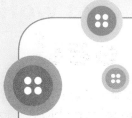

Stitches

There are lots of different sewing stitches to learn, and you will need to use different kinds for each project.

Some of the stitches may seem a little bit tricky at first, so it's a good idea to practise them on some scrap felt before you begin your project. Look out for Billy or Daisy giving you handy tips along the way! Ready?

Let's sew!

How to sew...
Straight Stitch

Straight Stitch (sometimes called Running Stitch) looks a dotted line. It is the easiest of all the stitches and can be used to join 2 pieces of fabric together, or even to "draw" shapes for decoration.

STEP 1

To start, bring your needle up from the underside of the fabric, then pull it all the way until you feel the knot tug. Then, a little way along, push the needle down through the fabric and pull all the way. Now you've made your first stitch! To secure your stitching, you always begin and end with a double stitch where you do 2 stitches on top of each other.

STEP 2

Now you can keep sewing — up, down, up, down, and so on. Make sure all your stitches are the same size and the same distance apart!

STEP 3

When you are ready to finish sewing, remember to do a double stitch at the end.

Tip!

For a quicker way of sewing Straight Stitch you can "weave" your needle in and out to do a couple of stitches at a time!

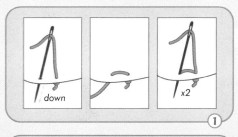

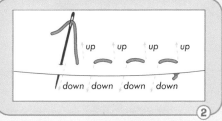

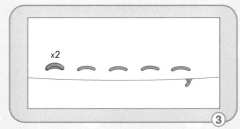

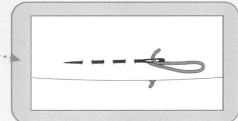

How to sew...
Blanket Stitch

Blanket Stitch is a traditional embroidery stitch used to decorate fabric edges. It works particularly well with felt or fleece, and looks great on cushions, scarves and lots more!

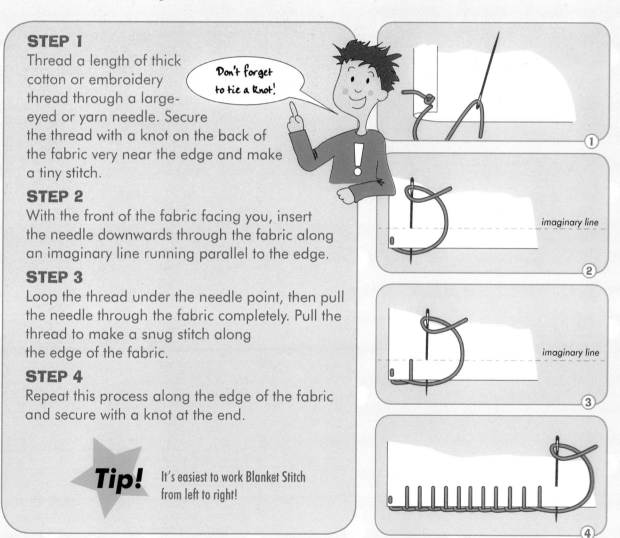

STEP 1
Thread a length of thick cotton or embroidery thread through a large-eyed or yarn needle. Secure the thread with a knot on the back of the fabric very near the edge and make a tiny stitch.

Don't forget to tie a knot!

STEP 2
With the front of the fabric facing you, insert the needle downwards through the fabric along an imaginary line running parallel to the edge.

imaginary line

STEP 3
Loop the thread under the needle point, then pull the needle through the fabric completely. Pull the thread to make a snug stitch along the edge of the fabric.

imaginary line

STEP 4
Repeat this process along the edge of the fabric and secure with a knot at the end.

Tip! It's easiest to work Blanket Stitch from left to right!

How to sew...
Backstitch

Backstitch is the strongest hand stitch. It can be used to sew pieces of fabric together securely. Backstitch is like a dance — one step **back**, then two steps **forward**. Are you ready to dance?.

STEP 1
Tie a knot in the end of your thread, then insert your needle up from the back of your fabric at A. Move your needle **back** to B and insert it. Bring it forward underneath the fabric and out the front at C, in one smooth scoop.

STEP 2
Pull the thread through then go **back** and insert needle again at A.

One step back, two steps forward!

STEP 3
Bring the needle forward and out at D. So, you go back for one stitch to fill in the gap. Then bring it out one stitch **forward** to make a new gap. Continue backstitching by repeating Steps 1 and 2.

STEP 4
For your last stitch, go back to fill in the gap from G to F, but then only go one step **forward** to come back out again at G. Go back in again at F and out again at G to make a **double stitch** to secure the end.

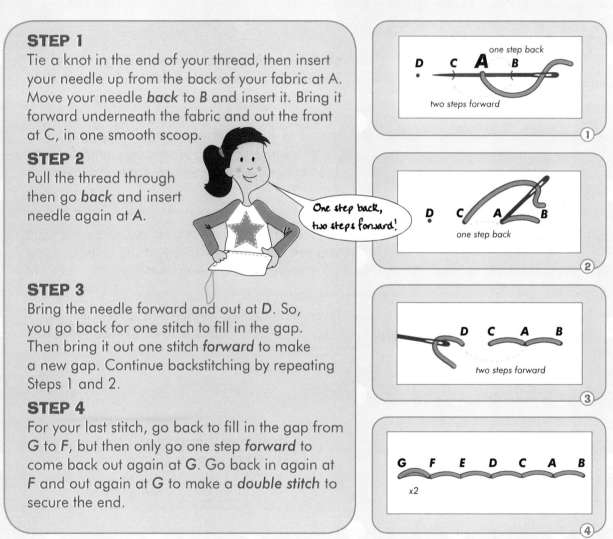

How to sew...
Overstitch & Slipstitch

Overstitch is a very easy stitch and can be used instead of Straight or Blanket Stitch to sew 2 layers together, or to close up gaps in a stuffed toy or pillow.

STEP 1
First, hide your knot by putting your needle in between the 2 layers of fabric and bringing it out where your first stitch will start.

STEP 2
Now loop around and bring your needle through the 2 layers and back out through the same spot. Do this twice to start, then move your needle up a bit each time to make a new stitch. Finish with a double stitch.

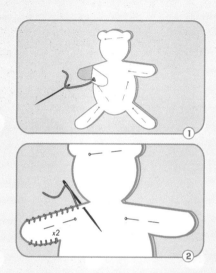

Slipstitch — For stuffed toys or pillows sewn on a machine or in backstitch, then turned inside out and stuffed, you can use tiny slipstitches to close up the gap very neatly.

STEP 1
First start at one end of the gap and bring your needle from the *inside* of the gap and pull it all the way to the *outside*. This will hide your knot!

STEP 2
Now bring your needle from the *inside* of the piece of fabric, *side 2*, and pull through to the outside like a zigzag! Continue with tiny slip stitches — inside to out, *side 1*, inside to out, *side 2* and so on, all along the gap.

Tip!
Don't forget to begin and end with a double stitch!

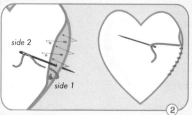

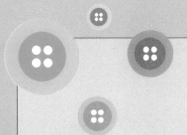

Things to make

Now that you've mastered your Skills and Stitches you can make just about anything! Here are some fun projects to get you started — which project will you make first?

House Needlecase

Stitches: Overstitch, Straight Stitch
Skills: Using a pattern, using pins, sewing on a button
Materials: Felt in various colours

STEP 1

Place the house pattern on a folded piece of felt and cut out. Do not cut along the fold, so that your house shape will be 2 houses joined together at one side. Then cut out the 4 windows, door and roof in other colours.

STEP 2

Overstitch the roof, door and windows to the front of the house.

STEP 3

Now cut another double house shape in a different colour felt for the inside of your needlecase. Place inside the cover and use Straight Stitch to sew the two layers together.

STEP 4

Fold the the house over.Use the inner felt layers for your pins and needles. Now they have a lovely new home!

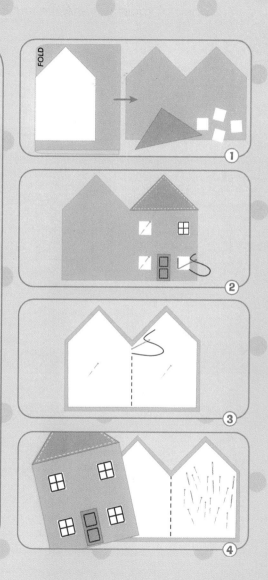

Cupcake Pincushion

Stitches: Overstitch
Skills: Pinning, cutting out shapes
Materials: Felt squares, embroidery thread, beads

STEP 1

Trace off the cupcake patterns (p.36). Cut out 2 cupcake shapes from some coloured felt. Then cut 1 icing shape from a different coloured felt or from printed fabric.

STEP 2

If you are using felt, sew some beads onto the icing. If you are using printed fabric for the icing you can forget this step.

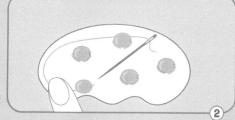

STEP 3

Pin the 2 layers of felt for the cupcake together. Pin the icing in place, on top of the 2 layers of cupcake felt.

STEP 4

Straight stitch around round the cupcake shape, and through the icing layer too, and leave a small space so you can stuff the cupcake then stuff it and Slipstitch the gap to close it.

Yum! Looks good enough to eat!

Flower Brooch

Stitches: Straight stitch
Skills: Using patterns, sewing on a button
Materials: Various felts, fabrics, ribbons and buttons, safety or brooch pin

STEP 1
Cut out your flower shape pattern from a piece of felt. This will form the back of your brooch. Now cut out lots of leaf shapes from different coloured or patterned fabrics.

STEP 2
Start sewing the leaf shapes onto the felt backing, with your stitches all being hidden in the middle of the flower. Add as many leaves as you like until you have made a pretty flower.

STEP 3
Then sew a button onto the middle of the brooch to hide all the stitches. You can also add beads or stitches to some of the leaves to make them pretty.

STEP 4
Now Overstitch a brooch pin or safety pin to the back of the brooch felt. Your brooch is now ready to wear! Why not make one for every outfit?

Crazy Creatures

Stitches: Straight Stitch, Cross Stitch
Skills: Using a pattern, using pins, sewing on a button
Materials: Felt, scraps of fabric, buttons and stuffing

STEP 1
Draw your very own crazy creature on a piece of paper to make a pattern, pin the pattern to 2 layers of felt and cut out.

STEP 2
Now cut out fabric for his eyes, mouth and teeth and sew onto 1 of the pieces of his body. You can use all sorts of stitches to make scars or tummy buttons, or to decorate their eyes and mouths!

STEP 3
Pin and sew the 2 body parts together, but remember to leave a small gap for you to stuff your creature. Once stuffed, finish sewing up.

STEP 4
You can also make small aliens and creatures to use as bag charms and keychains — just sew on some ribbon or a keychain to the back of his head. How many different crazy creatures can you create?

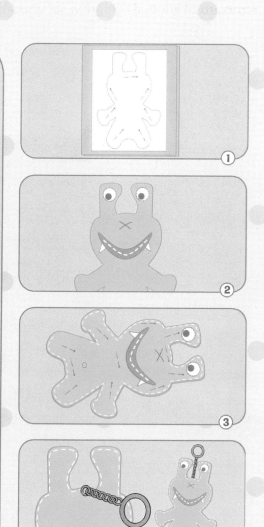

Hanging Hearts

Stitches: Straight Stitch, Blanket Stitch, Slipstitch
Skills: Using a pattern, using pins, sewing on a button
Materials: A selection of pretty felts and fabrics, stuffing, ribbons for hanging, buttons to decorate

STEP 1

For each heart, fold your fabric and use
the heart pattern to trace and then cut out
2 heart shapes from felt or printed fabric.

STEP 2

Now sew on smaller heart shapes, ribbons or
buttons, to decorate 1 of the heart pieces.

STEP 3

Now pin both of your heart pieces together,
and use Straight Stitch or Blanket Stitch to sew
around the edge. Leave a gap to stuff your heart
before you finish sewing it up with Slipstitch!

STEP 4

Now sew some ribbon at the top to hang your
heart from

I LOVE making these cool hearts!

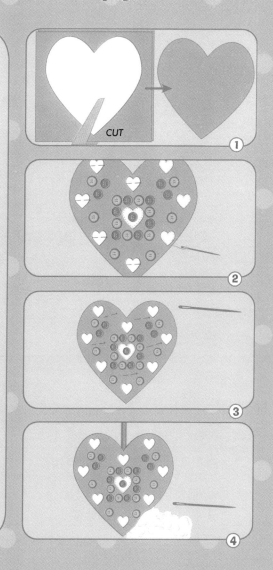

Birdy Garland

Stitches: Straight Stitch, Blanket Stitch

Skills: Using a pattern, using pins, sewing on a button

Materials: Felts and fabrics for the birds, stuffing, buttons to decorate, ribbon for hanging

STEP 1

Fold your piece of fabric so that the right side is facing up. Use the birdy template to cut 2 bird shapes from the same piece of fabric. Repeat for each bird, using different fabrics.

STEP 2

Decorate the top layer of each bird, adding eyes, wings and so on.

STEP 3

Now pin and sew each bird together, stuffing them before you finish sewing them up. You can use Straight Stitch or Blanket Stitch.

STEP 4

Now spread out your ribbon and pin your birds at regular intervals on it, then sew the ribbon onto the back of each birdy.

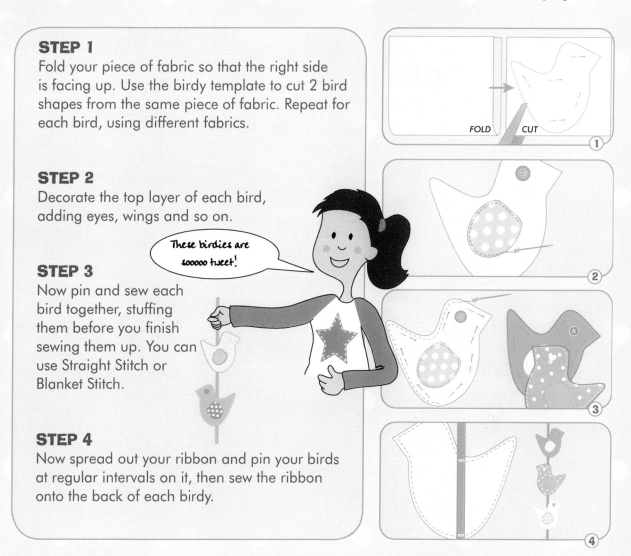

Cupcake & Birdy Patterns

ICING

CUPCAKE

BIRD
x2

Hearts & Flower Patterns

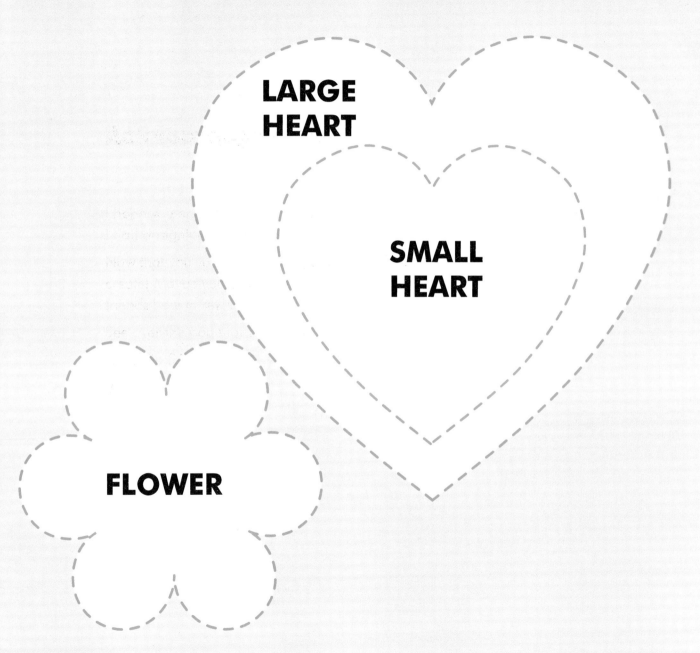

LARGE HEART

SMALL HEART

FLOWER

House Pattern

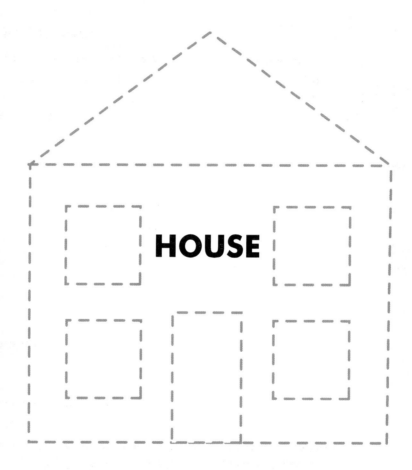

HOUSE

Acknowledgments

I hope you enjoyed this book, and had as much fun making the projects as I had designing them!!

Now that you've started to sew, there's no limit to the cool things you can create! Maybe you could even pass on your skills and teach some of your friends how to sew too?

See over the page for more books in my fab "Learn To Sew: Kids" series...

Keep On Stitching !

Alison

Learn to Sew: Kids

I hope you've had tons of fun learning to sew...why not add to your skills with my other books:

Learn To Sew: Kids
My First Hand Sewing Book

The perfect introduction to sewing for beginners. Follow Daisy Doublestitch and Billy Bobbin as they show you how to sew by hand and learn lots of easy stitches and sewing skills. Make super cool projects like Cupcake Pincushions, Crazy Creatures, Birdy Garlands, lovely Love Hearts and more!

Learn To Sew: Kids
More Hand Sewing Fun!

Add to your hand sewing skills with more great stitches and skills and make even more cool projects Kitten Slippers, Cute Cushions, Strawberry Purses, Tissue Monsters, Gingerbread men and more!

Learn To Sew: Kids
My First Sewing Machine

Get started with your first sewing machine with easy to follow illustrations and instructions! Learn all the parts of a machine and what they do, how to thread your machine and wind your bobbin, how to start and stop sewing, turn corners...AND make your first easy projects — cushions, bags, zip cases, skirts, i-pod cases and more! Sew much fun!

Made in the USA
Lexington, KY
04 March 2012